Daring to Share Your Story

An Authentic Journaling Guide

Companion to An Authentic Writing Guide

Diana Reyers & Tana Heminsley

DARING TO SHARE YOUR STORY

AN AUTHENTIC JOURNALING GUIDE

Diana Reyers & Tana Heminsley

 Daring to Share Global

Published by Diana Reyers and Tana Heminsley June, 2021
ISBN: 9781777548216

Copyright © 2021 by Diana Reyers and Tana Heminsley All rights reserved. No part of this publication may be reproduced, stored in or introduced into a retrieval system, or transmitted, in any form, or by any means (electronic, mechanical, photocopying, recording or otherwise) without the prior written permission of the publisher. This book is sold subject to the condition that it shall not, by way of trade or otherwise, be lent, resold, hired out, or otherwise circulated without the publisher's prior consent in any form of binding or cover other than that in which it is published and without a similar condition including this condition being imposed on the subsequent purchaser.

Editor: Diana Reyers
Typeset: Greg Salisbury
Book Cover Design: Olli Vidal

DISCLAIMER: Readers of this publication agree that, neither Diana Reyers, Tana Heminsley, or Daring to Share Global will be held responsible or liable for damages that may be alleged as resulting directly or indirectly from the use of this publication. Neither the lead publisher nor the self-publishing author can be held accountable for the information provided by, or actions, resulting from, accessing these resources.

By Tana Heminsley

Awaken Your Authentic Leadership:
Lead with Inner Clarity and Purpose
Awaken Your Authentic Leadership: Authenticity Journal

Awaken Your Authentic Leadership:
Authentic Leadership Conversations
for Meaningful Connection

EASE Amidst Challenging Times:
Simple Practices For Inner Peace Beyond COVID

www.LeadAuthentic.com

By Diana Reyers

Daring to Share
8 Brave Souls Sharing Their Authentic Road Trip - Volume 1
Tana Heminsley, Contributing Author

Daring to Share There to Here
2nd Edition | Volume 1
Tana Heminsley, Contributing Author

Daring to Share Trauma to Recovery
Special Edition 2019

Daring to Share Deception to Truth
Volume 2

Daring to Share Chaos to Calm:
Awakenings Through Covid
Special Edition 2020

Daring to Share Your Story:
An Authentic Writing Guide 2021

Daring to Share My Perception
Coming in 2021

Purchase Daring to Share Books | Become a Published Author

www.DaringToShare.com

PRAISE

The Daring to Share Your Story: An Authentic Writing Guide process seamlessly weaves Diana's deep expertise and sage voice together with time-tested tools and techniques in a unique and thought-provoking, yet approachable way. For me, it led to an entirely fresh outlook on my writing, inspired a renewed path of self-discovery, and reinforced support for my soul that I expect will endure long past the journaling experience.
~ Michelle Hohn

The Daring to Share program is a unique and supportive writing program. I learned to write from my heart, not my ego. It teaches forgiveness, kindness, non-judgement and helps you reveal your story from your soul. Diana is very supportive and helps guide you through your writing process from beginning to end. Along my writing journey, by following the guidelines in the workbook, my story just flowed and came from my heart. I highly recommend this writing program and will be forever grateful to Diana for her time, support and love. Diana's passion for writing is palpable and I thank her for helping me tell my story.

~ Maureen Rooney

Working with Diana has been a goal of mine since I saw her speaking at a Dare to Share event in 2018. Her compassion, empathy and her desire to bring people together for a better collective touched my heart in a beautiful way. The writing guide provided was a wonderful process and tool to allow me to "dig deep" while being supported in my self-discovery journey. Diana has been encouraging, caring, open and non-judgmental, qualities that helped me to gain the freedom that I needed to put feelings into words and how I wanted to really show up in the world with my words.

~ Julie Gauthier

I've always wanted to write a memoir and didn't know where to start. A friend invited me to join the book launch and Facebook Group, Daring to Share Your Story: An Authentic Writing Guide. I knew it was what I was looking for and ordered the book immediately. The step-by-step guide is easy to follow, very engaging and life-changing. Having the videos to refer and listen to provided clarity and ongoing support. I would recommend this work to anyone who is seeking to live a more authentic life. I felt it was the most valuable way to spend my time and money as I, like the rest of us, navigate and recalibrate through this pandemic.
~ Debra Rachar

I very much enjoyed the step-by-step, self-discovery, and writing master class with Diana Reyers of Daring to Share. The thorough videos, Tips from Tana, awakening exercises, journaling prompts, and coaching with writing really supported my path and deepened my understanding, helping me find my authentic voice. I found the weekly check-ins invaluable to the process, and encouragement from the team was really beneficial. I want to continue working with Diana as I continue to develop my writing style. I found the experience deep and delightful - life-changing. Highly recommended to any writer wanting to do this invaluable personal work.
~ Pamela MacDonald

JOURNALING STEPS

Journaling Step 1:   Understanding Authenticity 1
Journaling Step 2:   Discovering Your Values 11
Journaling Step 3:   Sharing Your Inner Purpose Feeling .. 21
Journaling Step 4:   Managing Your Inner Critic 31
Journaling Step 5:   Creating Inner Balance 41
Journaling Step 6:   Setting Boundaries 51
Journaling Step 7:   Integrating Centres of Intelligence 61
Journaling Step 8:   Having Authentic Conversations 71
Journaling Step 9:   Managing Inner Conflict 81
Journaling Step 10: Navigating Transitions 91
Journaling Step 11: Manifesting Abundance 101
Journaling Step 12: Visioning Your Next Step 111

INTRODUCTION

by Diana Reyers

Wherever you are is always the right place. There is never a need to fix anything, to hitch up the bootstraps of the soul and start at some higher place. Start right where you are.

~ Julia Cameron

I have spent over a decade consciously dedicating time and energy on elevating my self-awareness for the sole purpose of discovering how I can, integrally, show up in the world as the unique soul I have become.

It all started with a journaling practice – the morning pages to be exact - stumbling upon them in The Artist's Way Workbook by Julia Cameron. This daily practice changed my life, evolving into an inspired lifelong yearning to search deeper within my soul for the clarity I sought my whole life.

It turned out there was only one question I needed the answer to — who am I?

My first step was taking a bit of time every morning to have a conversation with myself through daily journaling. I then added self-discovery work, and the combination provided me with the awakening that I am very different from the person I thought I was expected to be. Moreover, that epiphany provided amplified relief to the degree that my soul felt free to be her authentic self with confidence and ease.

Yes, it is hard, uncomfortable, and sometimes fearful work. But, without taking that next step towards self-awareness, you will never know who you really are. And if you don't find out, you will never be able to articulate your true story. You have nothing to lose but yourself....

Enter the Daring to Share Your Story MasterClass Program. This self-discovery and writing program was created to support you to discover who you are as your authentic self while, simultaneously, writing your memoir to either publish or set on a shelf for family and friends to read in years to come.

Use this journaling guide on its own as your first step or delve into the complete MasterClass Program that includes the Daring to Share Your Story: An Authentic Writing Guide, this Journaling Guide, and my guided 12-part video series – you decide what you are ready for and the space and pace you need.

This is your time. I know this because there is never a wrong time for seeking, speaking, and being your truth. All you need to do is start one step at a time...

Each offering sold separately or as the complete
Daring to Share Your Story MasterClass package

www.daringtoshare.com

Discovering Your Authentic Story

Journaling Step 1

Daring to Share Authentic Learning

Showing up authentically includes being genuine and consistent in all parts of your life.

It requires using emotional intelligence to choose your response in each moment in line with your beliefs as you provide yourself with the time and energy needed to filter out judgments, assumptions, stories, and perceptions.

Learning to be aware of your emotions as they arise will support you to experience them, rather than block them when they are uncomfortable.

Being authentic allows you tap into your intuition to sense what you really want to say, do, and be - it supports you to manifest your way of being in ways congruent with your authentic-self or essence.

An Authentic Journaling Guide

Journaling Step 1

An Authentic Journaling Guide

Journaling Step 1

An Authentic Journaling Guide

Journaling Step 1

An Authentic Journaling Guide

Excerpt From Daring to Share There to Here
2nd Edition | Volume 1

Love is something that I find incredibly complicated because it isn't a tangible, black or white, all or nothing kind of item that is predictable or constant, but rather an ever-changing feeling that moves with the ebb and flow of my personal evolution.

~ Diana Reyers

Living and Writing Congruent With Your Values

Journaling Step 2

Daring to Share Authentic Learning

Understanding and living in line with your values and trusting how you feel provides you with internal guidance and intrinsic motivation. It supports you to live decisively during times when you are unsure of your next step. You can bring your values out and consider how you truly want to live your life and write within their context in your story. Being clear about your values and how you feel within them will provide guideposts for articulating boundaries you may need to create and for conversations you may need to have to live and write congruent with them.

An Authentic Journaling Guide

Journaling Step 2

An Authentic Journaling Guide

Journaling Step 2

An Authentic Journaling Guide

Journaling Step 2

An Authentic Journaling Guide

Excerpt From Daring to Share There to Here
2nd Edition | Volume 1

I was devastated. It was beautiful. I wanted to believe everything he said to me, but I felt damaged, and I went home and cried in the dark for hours.

~ Scott De Freitas-Graff

Sharing Your Story Guided By Your Inner Purpose Feeling

Journaling Step 3

Daring to Share Authentic Learning

When you choose to fully feel, both physically and emotionally, you give yourself the ability to be present and curious about why you feel the way you do. To provide more ease, narrow down your values' emotional feelings to just one that resonates with you. This is your Inner Purpose Feeling. It is the one emotion that encompasses all of your values and how you feel when you are living in line with all of them simultaneously. This is what it would feel like if you were living as your authentic or best-self most of the time. How amazing would that be?!

An Authentic Journaling Guide

Journaling Step 3

An Authentic Journaling Guide

Journaling Step 3

An Authentic Journaling Guide

Journaling Step 3

An Authentic Journaling Guide

INNER PURPOSE
FEELING

Excerpt from Daring to Share Deception to Truth Volume 2

When I pay attention to how I feel, I am able to tap into this world of new direction. By choosing to trust it and using it as a guide, I experience life on an entirely different level where connections to those around me run deep, synchronicity becomes the norm,
and everything I dream about unfolds as reality.
I know this is quite a declaration, but I voice it with confidence because I have experienced it, and I live true to it on a daily basis.

~ Chelsey Marie

Managing Your Inner Critic In Life And On The Page

Journaling Step 4

Daring to Share Authentic Learning

Befriending the inner critic allows you to utilize its messages with the intention to accept every aspect of yourself. When you find clarity about what your inner critic is saying, you have the ability to believe it or not. Over time, you can build the capacity to see the inner critic for what it is – it's really just a fleeting thought – one that lasts a few seconds and then goes away… if you allow it to…

At each moment, you can be empowered with the choice to agree or disagree given your level of awareness.

An Authentic Journaling Guide

Journaling Step 4

An Authentic Journaling Guide

Journaling Step 4

An Authentic Journaling Guide

Journaling Step 4

An Authentic Journaling Guide

Excerpt from Daring to Share Chaos to Calm Awakenings Through Covid Special Edition 2020

I feel out of control.
I feel alone.
I feel uncomfortable.
I feel out of place.
I feel fat....even though fat is not a feeling.

~ Julie Gauthier

Using Inner Balance to Inspire A Mindset of Truth

Journaling Step 5

Daring to Share Authentic Learning

Being emotionally intelligent requires having clarity about your authentic way of being – who you are when choosing what you say, what you do, and how you respond to others and situations from your essence. This, in turn, requires a deep understanding of which characteristics resonate with you, so you have the choice to show up within those that serve you well. When you choose to assess the behaviours of others and everything around you, you are able to establish how you want to respond to them authentically, and that can provide you with a balanced inner state of being, or inner balance, showing up in line with your personal integrity.

An Authentic Journaling Guide

Journaling Step 5

An Authentic Journaling Guide

Journaling Step 5

An Authentic Journaling Guide

Journaling Step 5

An Authentic Journaling Guide

Excerpt from Daring to Share Chaos to Calm Awakenings Through Covid Special Edition 2020

My story is one of the billions of victorious stories, and I am choosing to embrace all the challenges I have overcome in celebration of the semblance of balance I achieved moving through them.

~ Bristol Debowski

BOUNDARIES

Setting Boundaries To Create Space

Journaling Step 6

Daring to Share Authentic Learning

Setting boundaries provides the opportunity to live true to your authentic purpose and passion while honouring the same for others. Deciding to set a boundary, becoming aware of the momentary discomfort that might appear, and then practicing emotional and social intelligence will support you to discover how you can move forward with confidence and ease. Take your newfound decision-making skills to practice inner balance with the intention to show up as an advocate of self and others as you strive for the happiness that is your birthright.

An Authentic Journaling Guide

_____
_____
_____
_____
_____
_____
_____
_____
_____
_____
_____
_____
_____
_____
_____
_____
_____
_____
_____
_____
_____
_____

Journaling Step 6

An Authentic Journaling Guide

Journaling Step 6

An Authentic Journaling Guide

Journaling Step 6

An Authentic Journaling Guide

Excerpt from Daring to Share Deception to Truth Volume 2

I found myself surrounded by the deepest of maroon and engulfed
Inside a space I could barely describe with words.
My body felt warm and safe, yet I was frightened
as if I were a child again.

~ Elle Anna Nadeau

Integrating Your Three Centres of Intelligence For Inspiration

Journaling Step 7

Daring to Share Authentic Learning

Listening to and integrating your three centers of intelligence in every moment connects you to your authentic self, and essentially, your essence through the creative free-flow mode of thinking or being. You can let your Inner Purpose Feeling – your soul - freely guide you to your passion and purpose in life as you discover who you are and what is truly important to you.
You become awakened to the present moment, cultivating the quality of presence.

An Authentic Journaling Guide

Journaling Step 7

An Authentic Journaling Guide

Journaling Step 7

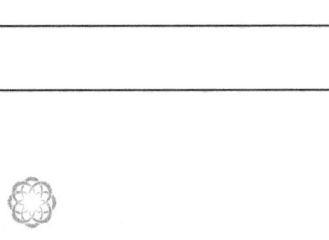

An Authentic Journaling Guide

Journaling Step 7

An Authentic Journaling Guide

Excerpt from Daring to Share There to Here
2nd Edition | Volume 1

I could feel myself digging deeper into a hole, and I knew something was wrong with how I felt about myself, life, and in particular, the way my mind worked against me. I just didn't know how to change any of it. I yearned to lift myself out of the hole early on, so I decided to try out a few things to see which ones felt right for me.

~ Tana Heminsley

Having Authentic Conversations While Sharing Your Story

Journaling Step 8

Daring to Share Authentic Learning

Utilizing your self-discovery this far will greatly help you understand your inner-self and be clear about how you want to communicate what you believe, how you feel, and how you wish to move forward and show up with others. It will support you to receive and process communication from others and then respond in a way that honours both conversation participants. Becoming aware of the inner landscape of your physical cues and your emotions and thoughts will support you to respond authentically at the moment. You can then use the information provided with awareness when in conversation with others.

An Authentic Journaling Guide

Journaling Step 8

An Authentic Journaling Guide

Journaling Step 8

An Authentic Journaling Guide

Journaling Step 8

An Authentic Journaling Guide

Excerpt From Daring to Share There to Here
2nd Edition | Volume 1

One might think that this story concludes with the uncovering of the gifts of acceptance and gratitude I received. However, I found that with each piece of healing, yet another opportunity of growth presented itself.

~ Donna Fitzgerald

Managing Inner Conflict While Reflecting On Your Truth

Journaling Step 9

Daring to Share Authentic Learning

Accepting that conflict is something that comes up over and over in your life will shift you view of its experience. It is a natural part of life as every relationship includes unique personalities, differing values, and ways of interpreting situations. This means that you aren't always going to agree, and you aren't always going to get along.

What matters is how you think about conflict and practice managing it.

An Authentic Journaling Guide

Journaling Step 9

An Authentic Journaling Guide

Journaling Step 9

An Authentic Journaling Guide

Journaling Step 9

An Authentic Journaling Guide

INNER CONFLICT

Excerpt From Daring to Share Deception to Truth Volume 2

I began to confidently recognize that I was my true authentic self when I gave all of me to my family, being half in just did not seem to work! I was fortunate to have the choice to be all in as a mother and not work outside the house, and my journaling allowed me to find clarity about why I questioned committing to what I knew was right for me.

~ Angela Allen

Navigating Transitions Through Your Life and Story

Journaling Step 10

Daring to Share Authentic Learning

Transitions present in many ways in our life. One often thinks of change as something planned for, but it also pops up suddenly in response to an adverse or favourable event that occurs or through the process of personally evolving. Moving through transition provides growth and, ultimately, wisdom. You can experience great discomfort within it, but if you tap into your resilience, you have the ability to land in a place of authentic comfort.

An Authentic Journaling Guide

Journaling Step 10

An Authentic Journaling Guide

Journaling Step 10

An Authentic Journaling Guide

Journaling Step 10

An Authentic Journaling Guide

TRANSITIONS

Excerpt From Daring to Share There to Here
2nd Edition | Volume 1

When I'm not aware, I am a pretzel,
and I will mold into what is around me.
I often wonder where my head was at back then.

~ Wendy Mah

Celebrating Abundance Within Your Life Story

Journaling Step 11

Daring to Share Authentic Learning

Maintaining an abundance mindset requires clarifying and manifesting what you want in life. Once clarity is established, you can confidently create a plan to move towards achieving your goals. Trusting your inner self is a key component in staying on your plan's course.

However, it is equally important to accept and manage any unplanned negative situations or experiences that appear along the way. Duality is the reality of life, and accepting trade-offs will help you achieve all you dream of and strive for.

An Authentic Journaling Guide

Journaling Step 11

An Authentic Journaling Guide

Journaling Step 11

An Authentic Journaling Guide

Journaling Step 11

An Authentic Journaling Guide

ABUNDANCE

Excerpt from Daring to Share Chaos to Calm Awakenings Through Covid Special Edition 2020

Experiencing the loss of my mother in childhood is my chaos, and 'gone too soon' is the definitive place where my deepest and darkest angst resides.

~ Michelle Hohn

VISIONING

Envisioning Your Next Authentic Chapter

Journaling Step 12

Daring to Share Authentic Learning

The Daring to Share: An Authentic Writing Guide process provides the gift of holding space for individuals to generate the power that has been forcibly hidden. Within that space, you may find you are not bound to the debilitating perception you had of yourself. You may find freedom in awareness of yourself and the world that inspires more compassion and connection. You may become empowered by getting your story out onto a page. Whatever it is that the self-discovery, journaling, and writing prompts within yourself, you will find a delicate balance of walking down the path that was made just for you.

~ Olivia Reyers

An Authentic Journaling Guide

_____
_____
_____
_____
_____
_____
_____
_____
_____
_____
_____
_____
_____
_____
_____
_____
_____
_____
_____
_____
_____

Journaling Step 12

An Authentic Journaling Guide

Journaling Step 12

An Authentic Journaling Guide

Journaling Step 12

An Authentic Journaling Guide

VISIONING

Excerpt from Daring to Share Chaos to Calm
Awakenings Through Covid Special Edition 2020

I am floating in a vast, beautiful, warm ocean, somehow silently and quietly pulled to the surface from the deep, dark depths below. I feel relief, I can breathe easy, and I feel the sun on my face, and the warm water gently washing over my body. I can finally catch my breath and stop treading water. Everything is a beautiful shade of turquoise and blue. I hear the breeze and feel it touch my body; the sun warms me as it sparkles above. This feels perfect, like love is touching me, comforting me. The water supports me as I float, no longer going under again and again, continuously trying to tread water. This is a new peaceful feeling;
I like it – it is what feeling calm must truly be like.

~ Michelle Shultz-Murphy

GREAT JOB!!
TIME FOR CAKE!!

ABOUT TANA HEMINSLEY

Tana is an Author, the Founder of Authentic Leadership Global™ as well as a retired, award-winning Leadership Coach.

She was awarded the *Vancouver Charter Chapter of the International Coach Federation's 2016 Coach Impact Award*. In 2019 she received the *CEO Magazine's Business Consultant Award* and was a *Book Excellence Awards Finalist* for her second book - *Awaken Your Authentic Leadership - Authenticity Journal*.

Tana has published three books in the *Awaken Your Authentic Leadership* series - about how to be your best self as an organizational leader. She has also written her first book for a broader audience titled *EASE Amidst Challenging Times: Simple Practices for Inner Peace Beyond COVID*.

She has spoken to audiences at hundreds of engagements and was a keynote speaker at the 2018 China Executive and Leadership Coaching Summit in Beijing.

Tana has more than 35 years of business and leadership experience, is a thought-leader in the area of Authentic Leadership and Emotional Intelligence and has been researching and practicing mindfulness for more than 15 years.

Tana lives in beautiful British Columbia, Canada, with her husband, Chris and cat, Buddy.

ABOUT DIANA REYERS

Diana Reyers is an Authentic Leadership Global™ Program and Conversation facilitator and the founder of Daring to Share Global.™

She began storytelling as a young child because it provided her with the ability to step into her uniqueness while fighting to fit into a world where extroverts are honoured and introverts are shamed. Through her teen years and well into adulthood, Diana lost herself, and at the age of 49, dug deep to re-introduce herself to her authenticity. Well into her personal work, she discovered the power of conversation and began sharing her story; she found a voice that people listened to while resonating with her stories.

Diana used her ability to share her story with her voice and through the written word in order to experience the genuine love that comes from feelings of acceptance and inclusion. By committing to and living in line with her values and beliefs, she felt the inspiring energy of connection and an unconditional sense of belonging.

Diana is a Human Advocate passionate about inspiring others to share their truth no matter how uncomfortable it may be. She knows that when we trust our story, we become empowered to share it and a spark of connection is ignited; the magic of storytelling takes us to compassion and empathy, and an amplified feeling of human-kindness is created.

www.ingramcontent.com/pod-product-compliance
Lightning Source LLC
Chambersburg PA
CBHW072202100526
44589CB00015B/2332